CONTENTS

Introduction   **4**

The Swan   **6**

The Rose   **8**

The Fortune   **10**

The first Globe   **12**

The second Globe   **14**

Indoor theatres   **16**

The theatre and the Court   **18**

Costumes   **20**

The symbolism of costumes and colours   **22**

Properties and stage setting   **24**

Style of acting   **26**

Rebuilding Shakespeare's Globe   **28**

Glossary   **30**

More books to read & Websites   **31**

Index   **32**

Any words appearing in the text in bold, **like this** are explained in the glossary.

INTRODUCTION

Williiam Shakespeare was a professional actor, a businessman, and a playwright. Today, nearly 400 years after his death, his plays are still performed, moving audiences to tears and to laughter. Shakespeare's works tell us much about **Elizabethan** England. What is most remarkable is that Shakespeare's plays can still tell us something about ourselves.

Shakespeare was born in Stratford-upon-Avon, England, in 1564. At the age of 18, he married Anne Hathaway. They had three children. Shakespeare then moved to London, the capital and largest city in England, apparently leaving his family behind. He wrote and acted in the London theatres during the 1590s and managed an acting company and a theatre building. He earned enough money at this time to buy the second largest house in Stratford, called New Place. His wife and children moved there in 1597. From then until his death in 1616, Shakespeare spent more time in Stratford. He continued to write plays that were performed in London.

Poets, players, companies

In Shakespeare's day, playwrights were called **poets**, actors were known as **players**, and theatres were known as **playhouses**. Shakespeare was one of several very gifted and interesting personalities of his time. English theatre had begun as travelling entertainment,

RIGHT: This engraving of William Shakespeare was made by Martin Droeshout in 1623.

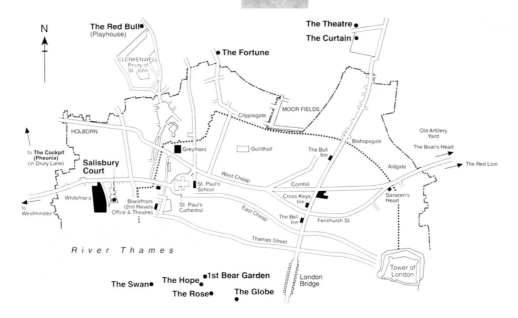

ABOVE: In the 1590s, London theatres were outside city limits.

in which groups of players set up temporary stages in inn yards or market places. Theatre became a fully professional activity and was held in permanent theatre buildings in the city of London. Players were forbidden by law to travel around as unattached entertainers. They had to form themselves into companies under the protection of a nobleman. Shakespeare worked for several different companies before becoming a co-manager and shareholder in the company called the Chamberlain's Men. When James I became king in 1603, after the death of Queen Elizabeth I, Shakespeare's company became the King's Men.

Playhouses

The first theatre building in London was probably The Red Lion, built in the Whitechapel area in 1567. In 1576, it was replaced by the Theatre in Shoreditch. The Theatre was built on one of the main roads going north out of the city. The man who built the Theatre was James Burbage. In 1599,

his sons, Cuthbert and Richard, reused the timbers of The Theatre to build the frame for The Globe. The Globe was one of several theatres on the south bank of the River Thames. This area was called Bankside. The Rose, in 1587; The Swan, 1595; The Hope, 1614; and a second Globe, in 1614, were all located on Bankside. The Fortune, in 1600, and The Curtain, 1577, were north of London. The Red Bull, which had been an inn until 1604, was in Clerkenwell to the northwest.

Audiences

Performances were given every afternoon, from Monday to Saturday. A fine day and a popular play would attract a large, mixed audience of as many as 3,000 people. One penny bought a place to stand next to the stage with hundreds of others. A higher price bought a seat in one of the **galleries**. The audiences included apprentices, tradesmen, scholars, noblemen, ambassadors, and foreign visitors.

THE SWAN

In 1589, Francis Langley, a successful London goldsmith, bought land south of the River Thames. In 1595 or 1596, he built a theatre there. In 1596, a Dutch visitor to London, Johannes de Witt, described the **playhouses** in his diary. Francis Langley's Swan theatre seems to have been his favourite.

There are four amphitheaters in London of notable beauty ... In them a different play is presented daily to the people. The two finest of these are situated to the southwest beyond the Thames ... Of all the theatres however the largest and most distinguished is that of which the sign is a swan ... since it has seating accommodation for three thousand persons and is built of a mass of flint stones and supported by wooden columns painted in ... excellent imitation of marble ... I have made a drawing of it.

A copy of de Witt's sketch (see opposite) was made by his friend Arend van Buchell in 1596, but the copy was not discovered until 1888.

De Witt's diary and drawing provide evidence of how the playhouses looked and how they were used. The playhouse buildings had a circular shape, an open roof, and a stage with space for an audience on three sides. Some spectators sat in the **galleries** and some stood in the yard. There are interesting details in de Witt's drawing, for example, the flag flying and someone blowing a trumpet in the tower. This may show that a performance was about to begin or was already underway. The three **players** seem to be dressed in clothes of their own time. They are placed well to the front of the stage. At the back is a covered area with two double doors for entrances. There are people sitting in the gallery above the stage. They might be members of the audience or musicians. It is likely that this gallery was also sometimes used as an acting area. Many plays written for the playhouses seem to need a room or space above the floor of the stage. Juliet's balcony in Shakespeare's play *Romeo and Juliet* is a famous example.

The Swan had an unusual past. The company that used it first, the Earl of Pembroke's Men, staged a play called *The Isle of Dogs* that angered the Privy Council. It was condemned as "contanynge very seditious and slanderous matter". In other words, the play criticized the authorities. The Queen's Privy Council immediately closed all the public playhouses. Those responsible for the play were imprisoned. For the remainder of Elizabeth's reign, only two companies were officially approved.

This incident shows that the playhouses were thought to have a powerful effect on public opinion. They were places full of dangerous ideas, as well as popular entertainment.

BELOW: This drawing of the Swan was made in 1596 by a Dutchman who was visiting London.

THE ROSE

E ven more detailed evidence has survived the years. It tells how the Rose, 1587, was built and managed. The Rose's owner and manager, Philip Henslowe, kept an account book and record of his business affairs. His books and records explain many of the financial arrangements of the theatre.

Henslowe entered into a Deed of Agreement with John Cholmley, a grocer. Cholmley was to pay a certain amount four times a year. In return for these payments, Cholmley could sell refreshments to the audience. He was entitled to keep the profits from the sale of "any breade or drinke". Henslowe paid for the construction of the theatre, but he and Cholmley agreed to share the job of finding the "**players** to use, exersyse and playe in the saide playe howse". They also intended to be present at performances so they each could keep on eye on their share of the ticket money, which they split evenly. In fact, their money came from only half of the sale of the **gallery** seats. The other half of the gallery seat sales and all of the penny-per-head sales from those in the yard went to the players.

From 1592, Henslowe's players at the Rose included Edward Alleyn, a leading actor, who had great success in the first performances of Christopher Marlowe's plays *Dr. Faustus, Tamburlaine*, and *The Jew of Malta*. Shakespeare's play *Titus Andronicus* had its first performance there in 1592, so it is possible that Alleyn played the title role.

LEFT: This 1626 painting shows Edward Alleyn, a leading actor with the Henslowe players.

In 1989, a team of archaeologists from the Museum of London unearthed the foundations of the Rose. The foundations show that the walls formed a polygon, which created a many-sided building on the outside and very nearly a circle on the inside. Five years after he first built the Rose, Henslowe improved it by adding a roof over the stage area, like the one shown in de Witt's drawing of the Swan. The new roof and the roof over the galleries was **thatched**. Henslowe also made his **playhouse** bigger by moving the stage back two metres (six and a half feet). The Rose Theatre Trust, which now looks after the site, intends to put the remains and artefacts on permanent display.

The rebuilding came at the time when Edward Alleyn was about to join the company. Henslowe seemed to be confident that he could now attract much bigger audiences than before.

The excavation of the stage has also suggested that the Rose had a different shaped stage from other theatres. It was 5.5 metres (18 feet) deep from the front to the back, and it tapered in width from 11 metres (36 feet) to about 6 metres (20 feet). The measurements of the stage of the Globe suggest that it was about 12 metres (40 feet) deep from front to back. A drawing still exists of a performance of *Titus Andronicus* at the Rose. The stage was small but for this play at least 17 people are needed for the first scene. It must have been a tight squeeze, both on the stage and behind it.

BELOW: This 20th-century model reconstructs the many-sided structure of the Rose.

THE FORTUNE

For 12 years, the Rose did well on Bankside. It attracted playgoers who crossed the London Bridge or took a boat over the River Thames to see the great actor Edward Alleyn in tragic or spectacular roles. Philip Henslowe and Alleyn both made a nice fortune. Alleyn retired from the stage and devoted himself to good works, which included the founding of Dulwich College, still in existence today.

The only serious rival of the Rose was the Theatre, run by James Burbage and a group of players that included William Shakespeare. The Theatre was north of the River Thames, a safe distance from the Rose. In 1599, the competition between the two theatres heated up. Burbage's sons had pulled down the Theatre and carried its timbers across the river to Bankside. They had employed an architect, Peter Street, to build a fine new **playhouse** close to Henslowe's Rose.

The new Globe must have been considered a serious threat, because Alleyn came out of retirement and leased a plot of land north of the River Thames in Cripplegate. Then he and Henslowe had Peter Street build a playhouse with all of the Globe's best features. They called it the Fortune. It was to be a state-of-the-art theatre that would re-establish the Henslowe-Alleyn theatre reputation.

The Fortune opened in 1600. It gained a reputation for being a disreputable place and attracted pickpockets and troublemakers. One of these troublemakers was Marion Frith, who liked to dress as a man. This gave her the freedom to go where she liked and to do as she pleased in the London taverns and playhouses. On one occasion she shocked respectable Londoners with a surprise appearance on stage. It was during a performance of a play by Thomas Dekker and Thomas Middleton called *The Roaring Girl*. The play was based on Marion's life. A Church court accused her of immoral behavior. An example of this immoral incident doesn't seem so shocking today.

… she sat upon the stage in public viewe of all the people … in man's apparel and played upon her lute and sange a song.

It would be another 50 years before actresses were accepted on stage in London to play women's parts.

The building contract for the Fortune still exists. It shows that it was a square building unlike the others. It had three stories and "gentlemen's roomes", which were boxes for the higher-paying members of the audience.

The stage was backed by a **tiring-house**. Its tower provided a space called the **heavens**, from which pieces of scenery, and perhaps even actors, could be lowered.

BELOW: An illustration of an Elizabethan playhouse shows the different levels that could be used for special effects, including lowering a player from the "heavens".

THE FIRST GLOBE

In 1598, Richard Burbage, the famous actor and theatre manager, had a problem. His father had taken out a lease on land to the north of the city where he had built the Theatre, one of London's first and most successful **playhouses**. The company of actors that played there, called the Chamberlain's Men, included William Shakespeare. Shakespeare shared in the running of the theatre and in its profits. As the lease came to an end, the landowner made it clear that he would not renew it.

Burbage made a brilliant and daring plan. On 28 December, 1598, he, his brother Cuthbert, and 12 workmen took axes and crowbars to the Theatre. They dismantled the Theatre plank by plank. They transported the timbers across the River Thames to Bankside. The river was frozen over that winter, so they probably pushed everything over the ice.

The Globe, which Peter Street built for Burbage, Shakespeare, and their colleagues, must be the most productive piece of recycling in theatrical history. At least 29 plays were written in 10 years for the Chamberlain's Men, who were later known as the King's Men. Shakespeare gave them 16 of those plays. In this recycled playhouse, Shakespeare's great tragedies were staged with Richard Burbage in the leading roles.

Plays for the company by other writers have also passed the test of time. Four hundred years later, they are still being performed around the world today.

BELOW: The actor Richard Burbage was the first to play many of the major roles in Shakespeare's plays. He played the roles of Richard III, Hamlet, King Lear, and Othello.

These include plays by Ben Jonson, in which Shakespeare was an actor, and plays by Thomas Dekker.

There is not much hard evidence about the structure of the Globe. But scholars have deduced some information from the plays that were written to be performed in it.

It took six months to build. It was round or polygonal on the outside and more or less round inside. The **galleries** had a **thatched** roof, which proved disastrous in 1613. That was when a piece of smoking wadding from a cannon used in a performance of *Henry VIII* flew across the stage and set fire to the dry grass of the thatched roof. The Globe burned to the ground.

In its brief life, the Globe must have been a lively place to visit. Its stage stretched well into the yard, bringing actors and audience close together. It had a large trapdoor, and above the stage, it had the **heavens**. The **tiring-house** at the back was an arrangement of a front wall with a door at each side for entrances and a central alcove concealed by a curtain or double doors. There was also an upper playing space provided by the gallery over the tiring-house.

The **players** could therefore create an interesting variety of exits and entrances. They could surprise their audience by disappearing below stage. They could reveal characters unexpectedly or fly in a special effect or an actor from the heavens. They could climb up to a balcony or appear on **battlements** by using the upper gallery. Musicians could also be placed in the gallery for a performance. And, because the audience was not far from the stage, they could make their favourable or unfavourable opinions very clear to the players.

BELOW: This in an illustration made in 1611 of the first Globe theatre.

THE SECOND GLOBE

After fire destroyed the first Globe, the partnership of shareholders immediately organized its rebuilding. These men had worked together since the formation of the Lord Chamberlain's Men in 1594. They were the Burbage brothers, Cuthbert and Richard; William Shakespeare; and four actors, Heminges, Condell, Ostler, and Underwood.

They had steered their company to considerable fame and fortune. Their confidence is shown by the fact that they raised more money between them to rebuild the Globe than had been spent on any other **playhouse** – £1,400. It was money well spent. The new theatre that opened in 1614 was described by an early visitor as "the fayrest that ever was in England".

Richard Burbage's father, James, had begun life as a carpenter before becoming a travelling **player** with the Earl of Leicester's Men. His stage would have been a simple, portable booth stage. James went on to run the first permanent playhouse, and his sons carried on the family tradition in the two Globe theatres. Both Globes were the most splendid and practical in London.

The second Globe continued in use long after the death of Shakespeare in 1616 and even after the death of Richard Burbage in 1619. It was

BELOW: Visscher's engraving of London, published in 1616, shows the Bear Garden and the Globe.

The Bear Gardne

The Globe

demolished in 1644 after an Act of Parliament in 1642 closed the playhouses.

The end of the Globe

… popular stage plays … are sinful, ungodly spectacles.

So wrote William Prynne in his book Histrio Mastix, published in 1632. Prynne was a **Puritan**, a member of a strict religious group that regarded pleasure of any kind as sinful.

The council for the City of London was dominated by Puritans throughout Shakespeare's career. They frequently made angry complaints about the corrupting effects of performances. If people saw murders on stage, wouldn't it make the people violent? If servants were seen tricking their masters, wouldn't the audience become criminal, too? This was the Puritan argument against the theatre. The Puritans were also anxious about the opportunities playgoing provided for pickpockets and prostitutes to follow their trades. They were also anxious about the spread of infectious diseases. And they were afraid that the large crowds at playhouses might become an unruly mob threatening law and order.

Shakespeare pokes fun at the Puritans in the character of Malvolio in *Twelfth Night*. Malvolio is a spoilsport who is ridiculed and tricked unmercifully by the other characters.

ABOVE: This 1647 engraving of the second Globe mistakenly identifies the building as **Beere Bayting**.

By 1642, England was on the brink of civil war. The Puritans were led by Oliver Cromwell, who opposed King Charles I. Parliament then had its chance to close down the theatres completely and to order the playhouses to be demolished. The Globe, where ambassadors and apprentices alike had seen the first performances of Shakespeare's plays, was forced to close.

Theatre was not part of English life again until after King Charles II returned to the throne in 1660.

INDOOR THEATRES

Since the 13th century, boys at the cathedral schools, the royal chapels, and the public schools had been performing plays. Their plays were often translations of Latin comedies. What started as an educational exercise became a popular and commercially successful venture. The boy **players** were the first to perform in indoor **playhouses**, and they attracted an enthusiastic audience.

James Burbage's Blackfriars theatre

James Burbage, the man who built the Theatre, was not a man to miss a trick. He had seen the success of the boys at their playhouse in Blackfriars, a fashionable residential part of London. In 1596, he bought a large hall in Blackfriars and converted it into a theatre for the Chamberlain's Men. This gave them a suitable place for winter performances. But local residents were not happy about having adult players on their doorsteps and tried hard to ban them.

There were six main indoor playhouses in London, but there is little detailed evidence about their size. The plays written for them, however, do provide some insight into how they were used, and some contemporary illustrations show how they might have looked.

LEFT: *Twelfth Night* was performed here, in Middle Temple Hall, in 1602.

Several points of difference from performances in the public playhouses stand out.

- The use of lighting by candles and torches.
- More ghostly and other special visual effects.
- More music, sometimes played for up to an hour before the play started, and played during the performance.
- More subtle forms of comedy, such as satire, which depended on a knowledgeable and sophisticated audience.
- Higher seat prices, which in effect meant that only the well-to-do could attend. Few tradesmen, and none of their apprentices would have been seen there.

Burbage's new playhouse was rectangular, with the stage at one end of a hall on the ground floor of the building. Most seats were in front of the stage, but there were boxes at each side and on the stage balcony. The upper **galleries** curved around, so the audience was on four sides. It is probable that the Blackfriars held 600–700 people; whereas the Globe held about 3,000. The Blackfriars also had 15 **gallants** on stools on the stage.

The increased admission charges went with the reorganization of the audience. Those who had paid the most sat nearest the stage. They sat at the front or in boxes at the side. Boxes are little cubicles separating the lord and his guests from the mass of the audience.

ABOVE: The Ballet Comique de la Royne of 1581 gives an indoor performance with lavish set decoration.

Most fashionable of all was a seat actually on the side of the stage. It was very popular with young noblemen who wanted to be seen. The glamour of the players rubbed off on them because they had to collect their stools from the **tiring-house** at the back of the stage. Playgoers paying the least amount sat at the back. This is still the arrangement in most theatres today.

The indoor playhouses served a more prosperous and fashionable audience than the outdoor theatres. From 1609, the King's Men played at the Blackfriars and the Globe. They continued to entertain the whole range of **Elizabethan** society. But the idea of playing to a selected audience had taken root for once and for all.

THE THEATRE AND THE COURT

Private performances

The companies enjoyed a third type of performance when they were invited to play at **Court** or in another great house, where they provided entertainment for the family's guests. Conditions here must have been similar to those in the indoor theatres, but these special occasions gave the opportunity for even more spectacular effects.

The Revels Office

Entertainment was an important part of life at Court, and in the reign of Elizabeth's father, Henry VIII, a **Revels Office** was set up to organize shows and maintain a wardrobe of costumes.

As the public theatre flourished during Elizabeth's reign, the Revels Office began to control all theatre matters. Parliament, or the government, was still in the early stages of its development, and the Queen's small, hand-picked group of advisors, called the Privy Council, was still the most powerful group. The chief officer was the Lord Chamberlain. **The Master of the Revels** and his Revels Office was directly responsible to the Lord Chamberlain.

BELOW: Plans for an indoor playhouse by Inigo Jones are possibly for the Cockpit, built in 1617.

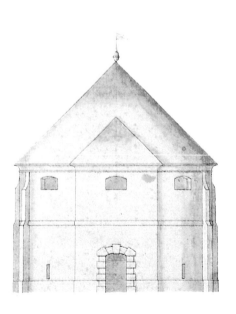

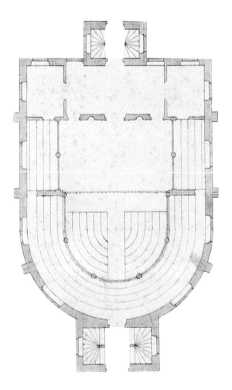

The Master of the Revels licenced companies and had the pick of performances for Court entertainment. He also censored plays. This meant that he could order sections to be cut out or performances banned if they were considered offensive to religious beliefs, or if they did not give unquestioning obedience to the rule of law, the Government, and the queen. Censorship by the Lord Chamberlain's Office in England continued until 1968.

Playing at Court

During Elizabeth's reign, performances were given in existing halls in the royal palaces, such as Hampton Court, Greenwich, Richmond, or Windsor. They were also given in theatre buildings that were constructed for special occasions.

The Great Hall at Hampton Court has a solid wooden screen standing 3.5 metres (11 feet 6 inches) in front of one of the end walls. Behind is a passageway leading to the kitchens. The screen has two doorways. A stage would have been built in front of the screen, and the doors covered with curtains to make a playing space similar to the stage in the public theatres. The queen sat on a platform at the opposite end with guests seated along the length of the hall, leaving a further playing space in the middle. The queen got the best view.

No expense or effort was spared in building a hall to honour and impress important foreign visitors. In 1581, the Duke of Alençon merited a specially

ABOVE: An illustration to the play *Roxana*, published in 1632, shows a performance taking place. The spectators seem to be sitting, suggesting an indoor playhouse, probably the Cockpit.

designed banqueting hall at Whitehall (now known as Banqueting House), where several plays were performed. It was highly decorated and included a canvas in the ceiling painted with clouds, stars, and sunbeams. Three hundred and seventy-five men worked on the hall. It was completed in three weeks and cost £1,744. This was an enormous amount of money for the time. A school teacher, for example, would have earned about £20 a year.

COSTUMES

The **Elizabethans** loved clothes. The queen set the trend for all those with the money to follow. They used rich fabrics decorated with lace, cloth of gold, and even jewels and pearls. Styles and colours changed as rapidly as they do today. The Elizabethans invented the names for the latest shades of colour, such as pepper, tobacco, seawater, and puke – a dark brown.

The **players** had to match the leaders of fashion in the richness and variety of their costumes for aristocratic characters. Thomas Platter, a Swiss visitor to the London theatres, noted in his diary in 1599 that noblemen often left their best clothes to their servants after their death. The servants benefited, not by wearing anything so grand themselves. It was against the law to dress in clothes intended for another rank in society. The servants would have sold them to the players. Philip Henslowe's and Edward Alleyn's papers show that they spent much more on costumes than on stage properties. The amounts are amazingly high. For instance, Henslowe bought a "black velvet cloak with sleeves embroidered all with silver and gold" for just over £20. People would have loved seeing all the wonderful clothes on display in the theatre.

Henslowe's list of costumes included

- cloaks in scarlet with gold lace and buttons
- cloaks in purple satin decorated with silver
- a costume in copper lace, "carnation" velvet, flame, ginger, red, and green
- women's gowns of white satin and cloth of gold.

RIGHT: Richard Tarleton was a very popular comic actor. Here he is dressed for a performance in a very simple costume with his pipe and drum.

It is as well that some players of poorer characters or servants could be simply and inexpensively dressed. They wore everyday clothes that they provided themselves.

Historical costumes

During Elizabeth's reign, performances were given in existing halls in the royal palaces, such as Hampton Court, Greenwich, Richmond, or Windsor. They were also given in theatre buildings that were constructed for special occasions.

Some people attending performances of Shakespeare's plays today say that they want to see them in the "proper dress". They dislike productions that use modern 20th-century costume or a mixture of styles. Yet the evidence suggests that Elizabethan players used basically "modern dress". They wore the clothes of their own time with additions to indicate special characteristics or a particular historical period. There is no evidence of much attempt at historical accuracy.

BELOW: This is the first known illustration of a Shakespeare play and shows an imagined moment in a performance of *Titus Andronicus*.

The Peacham drawing from about 1594, shows an imagined moment in a performance of *Titus Andronicus*, with the leading character dressed in a cloth, rather like a Roman toga, over the bodice and hose, or leggings. The soldiers with him, however, are in Elizabethan style. Henslowe's costume list is largely of contemporary Elizabethan styles, although of a rich, colourful, and decorated kind. He includes a small number of special items.

- two Danish suits
- one coat for a Moor
- four Turks' heads
- "the suit of motley for the Scotchman".

Players evidently enjoyed dressing up. Robert Greene, a **poet**, ridiculed them in *A Quip For An Upstart Courtier* (1592). Greene wrote that the player wore a fur-trimmed gown "laid thick on the sleeves with lace", and showed "his white taffeta hose and black silk stockings"; the huge ruff around his neck made it look as if his head was in a "wicker cage" topped by a "little hat with brims".

THE SYMBOLISM OF COSTUMES AND COLOURS

The **Elizabethans** had an interest in design of all kinds. They had a detailed sense of the connections between shape and colour and human experience. They also loved puzzles, clever jokes, and wit, including wit in choice of clothes. For an Elizabethan audience, the colours and styles of costumes worn on stage would have very specific associations.

An example of the use of colour is the costume for the character Hamlet from Shakespeare's play *Hamlet*. Hamlet wears black, the colour of sadness. Hamlet is mourning for his dead father. The colour yellow, the colour worn by a lover, causes problems for the character Malvolio, when he is tricked into wearing yellow stockings in *Twelfth Night*.

Doctors wore gowns of scarlet, lawyer's gowns were black, and serving men wore blue coats. A cardinal – an important Roman Catholic priest – wore rich scarlet, but a humble monk or **friar** wore a coarse **habit** of grey or brown.

Robert Armin, a popular actor in Shakespeare's company, wore a costume that had clear meaning for his audience. Instead of the fashionable short **doublet and hose** of a dashing young man, he is wearing the long coat of a "natural" fool, in other words, the coat of a simple, naive person.

Shakespeare's plays contain references to clothes, which emphasize their importance at the time. Polonius in *Hamlet* advises his son to make a good impression by dressing as well as he can, for "the apparel oft proclaims the man". Dogberry in *Much Ado About Nothing* boasts that he is a respectable, well-off man, because he is "one, moreover, that hath two coats".

RIGHT: Robert Armin, another popular clown, or comic actor, is dressed here in a long coat, which suggested to an Elizabethan audience that he was playing a fool.

Costumes in the Henslowe papers

The illustration to the right is of Edward Alleyn in one of his most admired roles, Tamburlaine, a character in Christopher Marlowe's play of the same name. Tamburlaine was a ruthless conqueror who lived in the 14th century. He rampaged around the eastern Mediterranean lands and died 183 years before Alleyn first played him on the stage of the Rose. Far from being dressed as a Scythian shepherd, which he first was, or dressed as the ruthless medieval warlord, which he later became, this Tamburlaine is elegantly dressed as an Elizabethan gentleman. The one piece of special costume is the decorated sleeveless **cloak** over his **jerkin**. Philip Henslowe's list of costumes included a coat with copper lace for Tamburlaine.

ABOVE: Edward Alleyn is shown dressed for the part of Tamburlaine in Christopher Marlowe's play. He wore rich Elizabethan clothing with a decorated, sleeveless cloak.

Henslowe's inventory

Henslowe's list includes some other exotic costumes: a "fairy's gown of buckram", which is a type of coarse cloth; "a pair of giant's hose", or leggings; and a ghost's suit. He also had in his wardrobe a bear's skin and head, a bull's head, a lion's skin, and two lion's heads. Shakespeare introduces a bear in *The Winter's Tale*, so presumably his company owned a bear skin, too.

Here are some of the costumes described in Henslowe's own words. Only the spelling has been modernized. A gown was a long, loose costume.

Gowns
1. Harry [Henry] VIII gown
2. the black velvet gown with white fur
3. a crimson robe striped with gold and faced with ermine, or white fur
4. one of **wrought** cloth of gold
5. one of red silk with gold buttons
6. a cardinal's gown
7. women's gowns
8. angel's silk.

Properties and Stage Setting

Stage properties, known simply as **props**, are all the things that are used on stage, such as tables, benches, bottles, and tankards in a tavern scene, or books and papers in an office scene. **Players** also had personal props, things particularly used by their characters.

Many of Shakespeare's characters need swords, daggers, or sticks. Prospero in *The Tempest* has his magic staff. The witches in *Macbeth* need a cauldron. Malvolio in *Twelfth Night* has to have a ring to give to Cesario. Players might have chosen other things that are not demanded by the **text**, but that help to show the personality of the character they play.

Shakespeare gives us a good idea of how props were used in the play-within-a-play in *A Midsummer Night's Dream*. Several workmen are to perform the tragic love story of *Pyramus* and *Thisbe*. The lovers are separated by a wall, and a player comes on suitably outfitted to play the part.

> *this loam and roughcast doth show*
> *That I am that same wall, the …*
> *truth is so.*

Someone in the company must have enjoyed himself mixing mud and plaster to make himself look like a piece of wall. In the same play, the Man-in-the-Moon has a dog, a lantern and a thorn bush, which are the traditional properties of this character.

Henslowe's inventory of stage and players' props

Thanks to Philip Henslowe's methodical list-making, the resources of his theatre company are known. Many of the things he itemizes must have been associated with particular plays. Henslowe lists "one Hell's mouth", which was probably used for performances of Marlowe's *Dr. Faustus*. His company continued to perform this at the Fortune after they had moved from the Rose, so it must have been a favourite with their audiences.

An eyewitness to a performance in 1620 gives a spectacular account.

> *a many may behold shagg-hayrd*
> *devils running roaring over the*
> *stage with squibs in their mouths,*
> *while drummers make thunder in*
> *the tiring-house…*

Henslowe's list includes small things, too, such as

> *1 globe … 1 pope's* **mitre** *…*
> *1 black dog … 2 fans of feathers …*

He also lists much larger pieces of scenery or construction, such as

> *the city of Rome … 1 chain of dragons … great horse … wheel and frame in the Siege of London …*

These things would have to be moved on and off the stage, as would the hanging man in the illustration from *The Spanish Tragedy*. Sometimes things could be "discovered" behind the curtain of the alcove of the **tiring-house**. Shakespeare's company performed *A Warning for Fair Women* in which a trapdoor was used to great effect.

> *Suddenly riseth up a great tree.*

The list of properties owned by the **Revels Office** is broadly similar to Henslowe's. The players must have enjoyed realistic detail and spectacular effects as part of their performances.

BELOW: An illustration to the play *The Spanish Tragedy* by Thomas Kyd shows a performance in which a flaming torch is used. The scenery is an arch from which a character has been hanged.

STYLE OF ACTING

The evidence for understanding how the **players** performed is found mainly in Philip Henslowe's papers, in the plays themselves, and in various accounts by members of the audience. There is quite a lot of information.

- Players were expected to attend a brief rehearsal period for a new play. They might be fined if they did not show up.

- Parts were written with the cues, or the lines spoken immediately before a particular character's speech, but no player would have had his own copy of the full play.

- There were no women on the **Elizabethan** stage. Women's parts were taken by boys or young men.

- Those playing the comic parts were notorious for improvising their own lines and jokes.

- There are many songs, dances, and fights in the plays, so players must have had these skills.

- Many performances ended with a lively dance called a jig. A Swiss traveller reported that even the "tragedy of the first emperor, Julius Caesar ended in a dance. They danced as was their custom, very elegantly; two people in men's clothes and two in women's combining wonderfully with each other, gave this performance".

- During performances, the players were helped by a bookkeeper or prompter, probably sitting in the **tiring-house** following the **text** in his copy. He also put up a plan of the action of the play, so that as players came offstage into the tiring-house, they could check what happens next.

RIGHT: Will Kempe is shown dancing a jig in this illustration from a story about his famous nine-day "dance" from London to Norwich. Jigs were a popular part of stage performances.

LEFT: These illustrations show the importance of gestures. Sir Richard Baker, an Elizabethan playgoer, was prompted to say, "Gracefulness of action is the greatest pleasure of a play".

Contemporary accounts

In Shakespeare's play, *Hamlet*, Prince Hamlet instructs a group of players on how they should perform. The Prince's warning about the danger of overacting probably reflects Shakespeare's own views. Hamlet wants the actors to have a fluent way of speaking and a moderate use of gesture with no shouting or overdone vocal effects.

Speak the speech, I pray you, as I pronounced it to you—trippingly on the tongue … Nor do not saw the air too much with your hand, thus, but use all gently … O, it offends me to the soul to hear a robustious fellow tear a passion to tatters … to split the ears of the **groundlings***.*

Hamlet also explains that the aim of acting is to show the audience what life and human emotion is actually like.

Suit the action to the word, the word to the action … For anything so overdone is from the purpose of playing, whose end was and is to hold as 'twere the mirror up to nature, to show virtue her own feature, scorn her own image …

A performance of Shakespeare's Othello by the King's Men in 1610 prompted a letter of praise. The writer particularly admired the skill of the boy playing Desdemona, Othello's wife.

They have acted with enormous applause to full houses … They had tragedies … in which some things … brought forth tears … Moreover that famous Desdemona killed before us by her husband, although she always acted her whole part supremely well, yet when she was killed she was even more moving, for when she fell back upon the bed she implored the pity of the spectators by her very face.

It seems that on this occasion the players of Shakespeare's company had achieved Hamlet's vision of the dramatic arts.

REBUILDING SHAKESPEARE'S GLOBE

On April 23, 1988, a fascinating and ambitious project began to take shape. A copy of the Globe Theatre, where Shakespeare worked for much of his career, was to be built. Sam Wanamaker, an American movie and stage actor with a passion for Shakespeare, was the man with the vision and the energy behind the project. There is a story, which happened years before 1988, of an enthusiastic American in a pub in the centre of London. This man was showing sketches to the customers and talking about his dream of rebuilding the Globe. Sam Wanamaker's plans were brewing for a long time.

Wanamaker had been raising support and money for several years before that day in April 1988 when the building began. Sadly, Sam Wanamaker died in 1993, before the project was completed. But he left a dedicated group of architects, theatre historians, musicians and many well-known actors, including his daughter Zoe Wanamaker to continue the project.

Sam Wanamaker's enthusiasm inspired support around the world. The organization he set up is called the International Shakespeare Globe Centre. The reconstructed theatre is not meant to be just a museum or an elaborate monument to a dead **poet**. Standing on the South Bank in London, near its original site, the International Shakespeare Globe Centre is a place for practical research.

BELOW: The modern Globe theatre in London is an accurate reconstruction of the original.

LEFT: The Swan is an indoor theatre in Stratford-upon-Avon, England.

Performances of Shakespeare's plays are given in conditions that mirror the **Elizabethan** theatre. There is natural light, live sound and music, an open roof, and an audience packed close to the stage.

Extensive research and historical detective work was needed before the new Globe's architect, Theo Crosby, could finalize his design. Sam Wanamaker praised the architect's skill at being the "chief negotiator between the demands of the scholars and the demands of practicality".

There are few surviving records or references to the Globe, and they are often contradictory. Was the theatre round, hexagonal – meaning six-sided – or polygonal – or many-sided? Was the stage in sunlight or shadow? Did some of the audience sit on the stage itself as they did in the indoor theatres? Key questions like this were explored.

The Globe project has no skeletons. [Its life] will not be a matter of resurrecting old bones, but of the excitement of modern discovery, a new life for old plays.

A few other theatres designed in the 20th century have tried to find the intimacy of the first **playhouses**. Most notable was the Royal Shakespeare Company's Swan theatre in Stratford-upon-Avon. Actors, directors, and designers working there discovered the challenges and opportunities of close links between the stage and an audience that is on three sides at stage level and in **galleries** above the actors' heads. The redevelopment of the Royal Shakespeare Theatre in Stratford looks rather like a larger version of the Swan. Elizabethan theatre gave and demanded an intense, energetic, and often highly charged relationship between performer and audience. Shakespeare's plays come alive in this act of sharing.

GLOSSARY

battlement decorative wall built to look like the defensive walls on the top of a tower

beere bayting bearbaiting; sport in which dogs fight a chained bear

cloak loose outer garment with or without sleeves

Court family, household, or followers of a king, queen, or member of the royal family

doublet and hose close-fitting jacket and long, tight trousers

Elizabethan relating to Queen Elizabeth I and her reign, 1533–1603

friar man who belongs to a brotherhood of the Roman Catholic Church

gallant man who wears showy, stylish clothes

gallery highest balcony in a theatre

groundling spectator who paid one penny to stand in the area of the theatre that is nearest to the stage

habit clothing worn by members of a religious group

heavens ceiling above the stage of an outdoor theatre, often painted blue with silver stars

jerkin short jacket without sleeves

Master of the Revels official who ran the Revels Office, responsible for approving and censoring plays

mitre tall, pointed, folded cap worn by the Pope, bishops, and abbots

player actor

playhouse theatre

poet writer of plays

props shortened form of stage properties, which are all things used on stage by actors, such as books, bags, and swords

Puritan member of a 16th and 17th century religious group who followed a strict moral code

Revels Office government office responsible for entertainment for the Royal Court text original words of a writer

thatch straw used as a roof

tiring-house theatre dressing room located behind the stage

wrought old form of the word worked, meaning "decorated"

More books to read

The Shakespeare library: Shakespeare: A life, 2nd edition, Wendy Greenhill and Paul Wignall (Heinemann Library, 2006)

Eyewitness Guides: Shakespeare, Peter Chrisp
(Dorling Kindersley, 2004)

Pronouncing Shakespeare: The Globe Experiment, David Crystal
(Cambridge University Press, 2005)

The Rough Guide to Shakespeare, Andrew Dickson
(Rough Guides, 2005)

Websites

These websites give a great deal of useful information:

www.shakespeare.org.uk
The website of the Shakespeare Birthplace Trust. Contains biographical information on Shakespeare and educational resources on his work.

www.rsc.org.uk
The website of the Royal Shakespeare Company. Includes a wealth of information about performances past and present.

www.shakespeares-globe.org
The website of the Globe Theatre in London. Features information about the building and performances. You can also find details of educational resources available.

Index

A
actors see players
Alençon, Duke of 19
Alleyn, Edward 8, 9, 10, 20, 23
Armin, Robert 22
audience 5, 17, 29

B
Bankside 5, 10, 12
Banqueting House, Whitehall 19
Blackfriars 16, 17
boy players 16
Buchell, Arend van 6
Burbage, Cuthbert 10, 13, 14
Burbage, James 5, 10, 14, 16

C
Chamberlain's Men, the 5, 12, 14, 16
Charles I, King 15
Charles II, King 15
Cholmley, John 8
Clerkenwell 5
Condell 14
Cripplegate 10
Curtain, the 5

D
Dekker, Thomas 10, 12
    The Roaring Girl 10
Dulwich College 10

E
Earl of Leicester's Men 14
Earl of Pembroke's Men 6
Elizabeth I, Queen 5, 6, 18–20

F
Fortune, the 5, 10, 24
Frith, Marion 10

G
Globe, the (first) 5, 10, 12, 13, 17

Globe, the (second) 5, 9, 14, 15
Greene, Robert 21

H
Hamlet 22, 27
Hampton Court 19
Hemminges 14
Henry VIII 13
Henry VIII, King 18
Henslowe, Philip 8–10, 20, 21, 23–26
Hope, the 5

I
International Shakespeare Globe Centre 28, 29
The Isle of Dogs 6

J
James I, King 5
jigs 26
Jonson, Ben 12
Julius Caesar 26

K
King's Men, the 5, 12, 17, 27
Kyd, Thomas
    The Spanish Tragedy 25

L
Langley, Frances 6
London 4, 5, 10, 15, 16, 28
Lord Chamberlain 18, 19

M
Macbeth 24
Marlowe, Christopher 8, 23, 24
    Dr. Faustus 8, 24
    The Jew of Malta 8
    Tamburlaine 8, 23
Master of the Revels 18, 19
Middleton, Thomas 10
    The Roaring Girl 10
    A Midsummer Night's Dream 24

Much Ado About Nothing 22
Museum of London 9

O
Ostler 14
Othello 27

P
Platter, Thomas 20
players 4, 5
Privy Council 6, 18
Prynne, William
    Histrio Mastix 15
Puritans 15

R
Red Bull, the 5
Red Lion, the 5
Revels Office 18, 25
Romeo and Juliet 6
Rose, the 5, 8, 9, 10, 23, 24

S
Shakespeare, William 4, 5, 8, 10, 12, 14, 15, 21, 24, 25, 27, 29
Shoreditch 5
Stratford-upon-Avon 4, 29
Street, Peter 10, 12
Swan, the 5, 6, 9

T
Tarleton, Richard 20
The Tempest 24
Theatre, the 5, 10, 12, 16
Titus Andronicus 8, 9, 21
Twelfth Night 15, 22, 24

U
Underwood 14

W
Wannamaker, Sam 28
The Winter's Tale 23
de Witt, Johannes 6
Whitechapel 5